SCIENCE
MAGIC
WITH FORCES

CHRIS OXLADE

BARRON'S

First edition for the United States, Canada, and the Philippines published 1995 by Barron's Educational Series, Inc.

Design
David West Children's Book Design
Designer
Siân Keogh
Editor
Jim Pipe
Illustrator
Peter Harper
Photographer
Roger Vlitos
Model maker
David Millea

© Aladdin Books Ltd. 1994
Created and designed by
N.W. Books
28 Percy Street
London W1P 9FF

First published in
Great Britain in 1994 by
Franklin Watts Ltd.
96 Leonard Street
London EC2A 4RH

All inquiries should be addressed to:
Barron's Educational Series, Inc.
250 Wireless Boulevard
Hauppauge, NY 11788

International Standard Book No.
0-8120-6502-6 (hardcover)
0-8120-9191-4 (paperback)

Library of Congress Catalog
Card No. 94-32052

Library of Congress Cataloging-in-Publication Data

Oxlade, Chris.
Science magic with forces / Chris Oxlade. — 1st ed. for the U.S., Canada, and the Philippines
p. cm. — (Science magic)
Includes index.
ISBN 0-8120-6502-6. — ISBN 0-8120-9191-4 (pbk.).
1. Conjuring—Juvenile literature.
2. Force and energy—Juvenile literature. 3. Scientific recreations—Juvenile literature. [1. Magic tricks. 2. Force and energy. 3. Scientific recreations.]
I. Title. II. Series.
GV 1548.0955 1994   94-32052
793.8—dc20   CIP
                                              AC

Printed in Belgium
4567 4208 987654321

CONTENTS

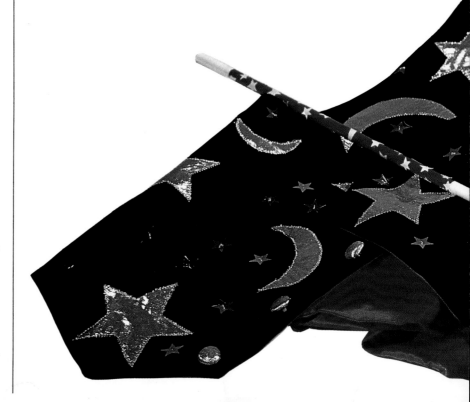

FORCES MAGIC!

Forces are all around us and come in many different forms. Without forces, we couldn't walk or breathe; in fact, we wouldn't exist in the first place! A force is anything that causes an object to change its motion or its shape. For example, when you ride a bicycle, you apply a force to make it move forward, and when you squeeze an orange, you apply a force to change its shape. Forces are usually invisible and silent – the perfect tool for the magician. May the forces be with you!

BE AN EXPERT MAGICIAN

PREPARING YOUR ROUTINE

There is much more to being a magician than just doing tricks. It is important that you and your assistant practice your whole routine many times, so that your performance goes smoothly when you do it for an audience. You will be a more entertaining magician if you do.

PROPS

Props are all the bits and pieces of equipment that a magician uses during an act including his or her clothes as well as the things needed for the tricks themselves. It's a good idea to make a magician's trunk from a large box to keep all your props in. During your routine, you can dip into the trunk, pulling out all sorts of equipment and crazy objects (see Misdirection). You could also tell jokes about these objects.

PROPS LIST

Magic wand ★ Top hat
Vest ★ Aluminum foil
Broomstick ★ Cardboard:
boxes, tubes, round box lids
Cellophane tape ★ Chairs ★ Colored
paper ★ Glue ★ Large die ★ Modeling
clay ★ Oil-based paint ★ Old curtain ★ Paints
Paper cups ★ Pencils ★ Rope ★ Round balloons
Rubber bands ★ Scissors ★ Scrap paper ★ Silk scarves
Small plastic trash bag ★ Sponge ★ String ★ Thin and thick
cardboard ★ Thumb tacks ★ Wooden board

WHICH TRICKS?

Decide which tricks you want to put in your routine. Put in some long tricks and some short tricks to keep your audience interested. If you can, include a trick that you can keep going back to during the routine. Magicians call this a "running gag."

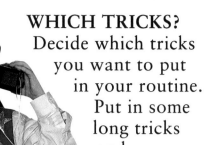

MAGICIAN'S PATTER

Patter is what you say during your routine. Good patter makes a routine much more interesting and allows it to run more smoothly. It is a good way

to entertain your audience during the slower parts of your routine. Try to make up a story for each trick. Remember to introduce yourself and your assistant at the start and to thank your audience at the end. Practice your patter when you practice your tricks.

MISDIRECTION

Misdirection is an important part of a magician's routine. By waving a colorful scarf in the air or telling a joke, you can distract an audience's attention from something you'd rather they didn't see!

KEEP IT SECRET

The best magicians never give away their secrets. If anyone asks how your tricks work, just reply, "By magic!" Then you can impress people with your tricks again and again.

INTRODUCING MAGIC MIKE
AND THE
TRICKY TOPPLER

Magic Mike uses his powers of mind over matter to make the toppler balance.

Start with the toppler right side up. Touch it with your magic wand and then balance it on the edge of the base. The audience will be surprised that it balances in this strange way. Now ask a member of your audience to try the trick, but first secretly turn the toppler upside down before you hand it to your volunteer.

WHAT YOU NEED
Cardboard boxes
Modeling clay
Aluminum foil
Colored paper ★ Glue
Cellophane tape

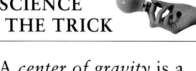

THE SCIENCE BEHIND THE TRICK

Center of gravity above other box

A *center of gravity* is a point through which the Earth's gravity appears to pull on an object. On the toppler it is near the weighted corner.

Center of gravity has nothing below it

The toppler will balance only if it is supported directly below its center of gravity. If it is not, it will fall over.

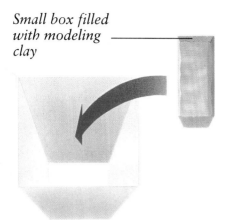

Small box filled with modeling clay

2 Put the small box into the bottom of the toppler. Press it firmly into place with pieces of cellophane tape.

Base box

1 Find a small box and fill it with modeling clay. Adding this extra weight to one corner of the tall thin box will shift the center of gravity toward that corner.

Weighted box taped to bottom and side

3 Make a low base from another box. Decorate both boxes with colored paper and add foil magic shapes and symbols.

WHAT YOU NEED
Cardboard box ★ Thumb tacks ★ Colored paper Paints ★ Scissors ★ Glue Cellophane tape Round balloons

INTRODUCING MAGIC MANDY
AND THE
BED OF NAILS

Incredibly the sharp points of the bed of nails do not burst Magic Mandy's balloon.

This trick is a good opportunity for some patter. "When I was in the Mystic East I saw a man lying on a bed of nails..." might be a good start. As you talk, blow up a balloon, tie a knot in its neck, and put it on the table. Give the bed of nails to your audience to see how sharp the thumb tacks are. Now press the box down on the balloon – nothing happens! Then burst the balloon with a single thumb tack.

THE SCIENCE
BEHIND THE TRICK

A sharp point bursts a balloon because all the force is concentrated at one tiny point, the end of the thumb tack.

Using the box, the force is spread out between the points so that each individual tack pushes into the balloon less.

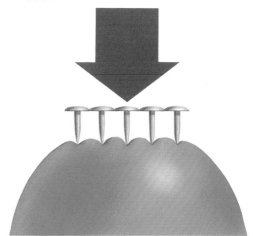

1 Find a small cardboard box. Open the box and carefully push the thumb tacks all the way through the bottom in a grid pattern. Glue them in place.

Thumb tacks arranged in a grid

2 Close the box again and seal the top down with cellophane tape. Decorate the box with magic shapes either cut from colored paper or painted on. Use round balloons, since these will work best.

INTRODUCING MAGIC MANDY
AND THE
SUPER STRONG MAGIC

Magic Mandy's monster wand gives her superhuman strength.

Tell your audience that your monster magic wand gives its owner the powers of superhuman strength. Hold one end of the wand and have a volunteer hold the other. Challenge your volunteer to push you over. Lift your end of the wand. No matter how hard your volunteer pushes, you will easily be able to remain standing upright.

WHAT YOU NEED
Broomstick ★ Paints
Colored paper ★ Glue
Scissors

THE SCIENCE
BEHIND THE TRICK

With the broomstick in a horizontal position the force of the volunteer's push on the wand pushes you. This makes you fall.

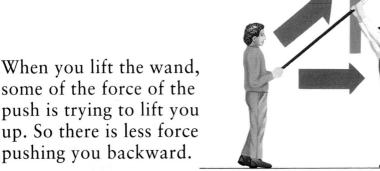

When you lift the wand, some of the force of the push is trying to lift you up. So there is less force pushing you backward.

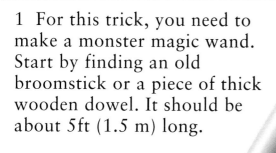

1 For this trick, you need to make a monster magic wand. Start by finding an old broomstick or a piece of thick wooden dowel. It should be about 5ft (1.5 m) long.

— *Broomstick*

2 Now decorate the broomstick to make it look like a magic wand. Paint the ends white and the middle black. Add magic shapes and symbols either cut from colored paper or painted on.

WARNING: When you lift the monster wand above your head, make sure your volunteer doesn't start pushing until you are ready, or they might accidentally poke you in the face!

INTRODUCING MAGIC MANDY
AND THE
WEIRD WAND

It's incredible! The weird wand seems to float in the air under Magic Mandy's spell.

Start by putting the two supporting boxes on the tabletop. Carefully rest the tube on the supports. Wave your wand over the tube. Now gradually slide the support out from under the end of the tube that does *not* contain the modeling clay. Amazingly the tube will not fall. However, if you remove the other support, the wand will fall.

WHAT YOU NEED
Cardboard tube
Modeling clay
Colored paper ★ Paints
Small cardboard boxes
or thin cardboard
Scrap paper ★ Glue

THE SCIENCE BEHIND THE TRICK

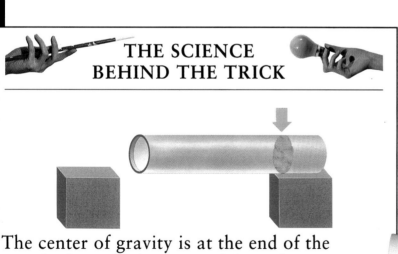

The center of gravity is at the end of the wand where the heavy modeling clay is. So it balances with just that end supported.

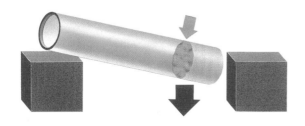

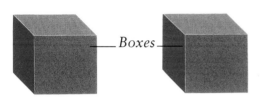

Tube   *Modeling clay*

1 Find a cardboard tube about 12in. (30 cm) long. Fill one end with modeling clay.

Boxes

2 Find two identical small cardboard boxes, or make them from thin cardboard.

3 Decorate the tube to look like a magic wand. Stuff the ends with paper. Decorate the boxes with magic symbols.

SPIN

Magic Mike's mysterious spinning top just keeps on spinning.

Ask for a volunteer from your audience to help with the trick. Give him or her the top with no weight inside and keep the heavier one for yourself. Now challenge your volunteer to spin the top so that it keeps going longer than yours. Armed with the magic spinning top you will always win.

WHAT YOU NEED
Round cardboard box lids ★ Modeling clay Pencils ★ Paints Colored paper Cellophane tape ★ Glue

THE SCIENCE BEHIND THE TRICK

The heavier the top, the greater the force needed to get it spinning and the longer it takes to slow down. Having the weight at the edges rather than in the middle also makes it spin longer.

Top with more weight spins longer

Top with less weight stops spinning sooner

Modeling clay *Lid*

1 Remove the lids from a box. Put modeling clay into the base as shown.

Tape

2 Seal the lid with cellophane tape. Make a mark at the center of the lid with a pencil.

3 Carefully push a pencil through the center to make a spinning top. Make another top with no weight in it. Decorate them.

17

INTRODUCING MAGIC MIKE
AND THE
TOPPLING TOWER

Surely it's impossible! Magic Mike removes the bag without touching the tower.

Put the plastic trash bag on the table. Gradually build a tower of boxes on top of it. Explain the trick to your audience as you build. Announce that you can remove the plastic bag without touching or moving the tower. Hold the corners of the plastic bag and pull it out straight along the table with a sharp tug. You will have to practice this trick many times before you try it with an audience.

WHAT YOU NEED
Small cardboard boxes
Modeling clay ★ Colored
paper ★ Small plastic
trash bag ★ Tape
Paints ★ Glue

THE SCIENCE
BEHIND THE TRICK

There are two reasons why this trick works: (1) Gravity pulls on the boxes creating a downward force so that the boxes tend to stay where they are. This is called *inertia*. (2) By pulling the bag quickly you reduce the friction between the bag and the boxes.

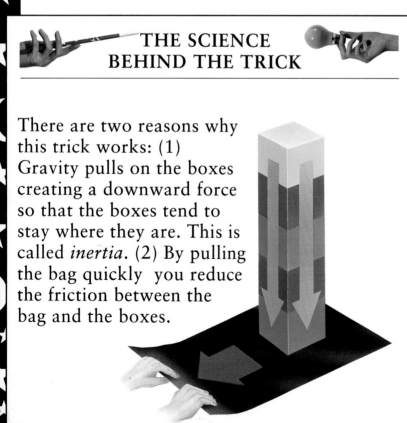

1 For this trick you need several small boxes. Put a layer of modeling clay into the bases to make them heavier.

Modeling clay

2 Close the boxes and tape them shut. Decorate each one with colored magic shapes and symbols.

INTRODUCING MAGIC MAXINE
AND THE
DISAPPEARING DICE

Magic Maxine spins the magic tube around her head and the die disappears!

Pick up the tube and show it to your audience so that they can see that the top compartment is empty. Now show them the die and drop it into the tube. Hold the tube by the string and swing it around and around. You should feel the die slide through the trap door into the bottom compartment. Stop swinging and show the "empty" tube.

WHAT YOU NEED
Die ★ Thin cardboard
Modeling clay ★ Glue
String ★ Cellophane tape
Scissors

THE SCIENCE
BEHIND THE TRICK

When you swing something (such as a bag of books) in a circle, you have to keep pulling on it. If you let go it flies off in a straight line.

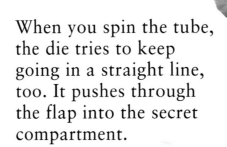

When you spin the tube, the die tries to keep going in a straight line, too. It pushes through the flap into the secret compartment.

1 Find a large die or make one from cardboard. Add modeling clay as weight if necessary. Make a rectangular cardboard tube by copying the shapes shown here onto a piece of thin cardboard. Cut them out and score along the dotted lines with the point of a pair of scissors. Glue the inside flap in place near the center and fold the cardboard into a rectangular tube.

The measurement for "x" should be 1/8 in. (4mm) bigger than for "y"

String

Bottom

Flap

Inside flap

2 Cut a piece of string about four times as long as the tube. Attach the ends of the string near the top of the tube with cellophane tape. Your tube is now ready to use.

INTRODUCING MAGIC MAURICE
AND THE
CUPS AND BALLS

Where is the silver? Only Magic Maurice knows the secret of the cups and balls.

Start with three cups in a line (we'll call them A, B and C), and one ball under A and one under B. Lift B by its base so that the ball stays on the table. Replace B over the ball. Lift A by the rim so that the ball stays in it. The audience will think it's empty. Also lift C to show it's empty too. Now tap the cups with your wand. Lift B by the rim. The ball is gone! Lift A by the base. There's the ball!

WHAT YOU NEED
Paper cups ★ Scrap paper ★ Aluminum foil Colored paper ★ Glue

THE SCIENCE BEHIND THE TRICK

Friction is a force that tries to stop things from sliding against each other. The more two things are pushed together, the greater the friction between them.

When you squeeze the sides of the cup, the friction between the cup and the ball becomes greater. It stops the ball from sliding out.

Ball held inside cup by squeezing cup

GETTING PREPARED

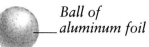

Plastic cup

Ball of aluminum foil

1 Make a paper ball and cover it with aluminum foil. It must fit neatly into the top of the cup.

2 Make another ball the same way and decorate the three paper cups with magic shapes.

INTRODUCING MAGIC MAURICE
AND THE
JUMPING PENCILS

Magic Maurice makes the pencils jump to attention at his command!

Put the cup on the table with the pencils inside. Lift them out one by one and hang them over the edge. Hold the cup in one hand in front of your face. Now announce that you can make the pencils jump back into the cup without touching them. Drop the cup and catch it with your other hand. Presto! The pencils will be inside the cup.

WHAT YOU NEED
Rubber bands ★ Scissors
Small pencils
Cellophane tape ★ Paper
cups ★ Paints ★ Colored
paper ★ Glue

THE SCIENCE
BEHIND THE TRICK

Force of Rubber band

When the pencil is hanging outside the cup, gravity is pulling it downward and the rubber band is pulling it upward. The rubber band pulls because it's stretched.

Force of gravity

When you drop the cup, it and the pencils begin to fall freely. They lose their weight and the rubber band pulls the pencils into the cup.

1 Cut four rubber bands so that you have four long pieces. Tape the top of each pencil to the end of each rubber band. Tape the other end of the rubber band inside the cup so that the rubber band is just stretched.

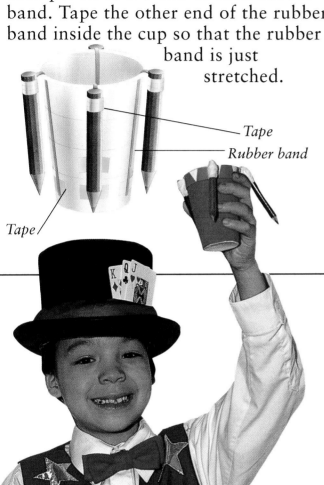

Tape

Rubber band

Tape

2 Decorate the cup with colored magic shapes or paint it with oil-based paints.

INTRODUCING MAGIC MAXINE
AND THE
FLOATING CHAIR

And finally! Magic Maxine summons all her power to make a person float in the air!

Start by asking for a volunteer from your audience. Make sure he or she likes flying! Sit your volunteer on the chair and ask him or her to sit as still as possible. Wave your wand around the chair and say some magic words. This is the signal to your hidden assistants to push down gently on the wooden board. Your volunteer will float into the air! Magicians call floating like this levitation.

WHAT YOU NEED
Three chairs ★ An old curtain ★ Wooden pole or rope ★ Scissors
A wooden board
Assistants

THE SCIENCE BEHIND THE TRICK

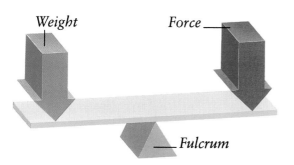

A lever is a long pole or wooden board on a pivot (called the fulcrum). The weights on each side of the fulcrum try to push the lever in different directions — up and down. In this picture the two weights balance each other.

The further the weight moves from the fulcrum, the more it tries to change the lever's direction. So the small push down on the board behind the curtain can balance the volunteer's weight on the chair.

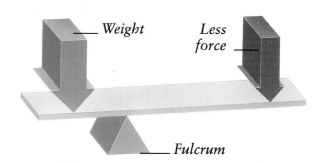

Curtain

Chairs

Wooden
board

Wooden board
attached to chair

Ask an adult to help you set up this trick to make sure it's safe. First, find three chairs that are sturdy and have seats that are the same height off the ground. Hang an old curtain on a wooden pole or over a rope. Cut a slot just level with the seats of the chairs. Put two chairs just behind the curtain as shown. Lay a wooden board across the chairs and slide its end through the slot and under the other chair.

HINTS AND TIPS

Here are some hints and tips for making your props. Good props will make your act look more professional, so spend time making and decorating your props, and look after them carefully. As well as the special props you need for each trick, try to make some general props such as a vest and a magic wand.

Decorate your props with magic shapes cut from colored paper. Paint bottles and tubes with oil-based paint.

You will need cellophane tape and glue to make props. Double-sided tape may also be useful. Thick fabric-based tape is good for joining the edges of boxes together, and it's easy to paint, too.

Stenciling is a good way to decorate large areas. Cut magic shapes such as stars and crescent moons out of cardboard. Throw away the shape, but keep the hole! Put the hole over your surface and paint through it with a sponge.

Your act will look more professional if you make a stage setting. This is easy if you have a backdrop to hang behind the stage. A large piece of black cloth is most effective. Use silver paint to create stars and moons. Also decorate pieces of cloth to throw over your table. The overall effect will be dramatic, creating an atmosphere of mystery and magic.

Make your own magician's clothes. Try to find an old hat and vest to decorate. If you can find some silvery material, cut out stars and moons and sew them on. An alternative is to use sequins, or anything else that is shiny and dramatic so you look professional.

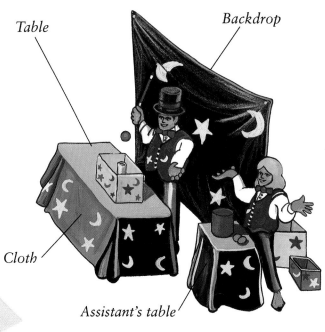

Table

Backdrop

Cloth

Assistant's table

Make a magician's table by draping a cloth over an ordinary table. You can put the props out of sight underneath.

GLOSSARY

CENTER OF GRAVITY The location in an object where the force of gravity appears to act. If an object is supported from any point below the center of gravity, the object will remain upright. But if the support is to one side of the center of gravity, the object will topple over.

FORCE Any cause that changes the motion or the shape of an object.

FRICTION The force that resists movement when one surface moves against another.

FULCRUM The pivot point of a lever.

GRAVITY The force that attracts objects to each other because of their mass. The more massive the object is, the greater its force of gravity.

INERTIA A property of all objects that makes a resting object remain still unless some force causes it to move. It also means that an object will continue to move at constant speed and direction unless some outside force changes the object's motion.

INDEX